To Burp or Not to Burp

A Guide to Your Body in Space

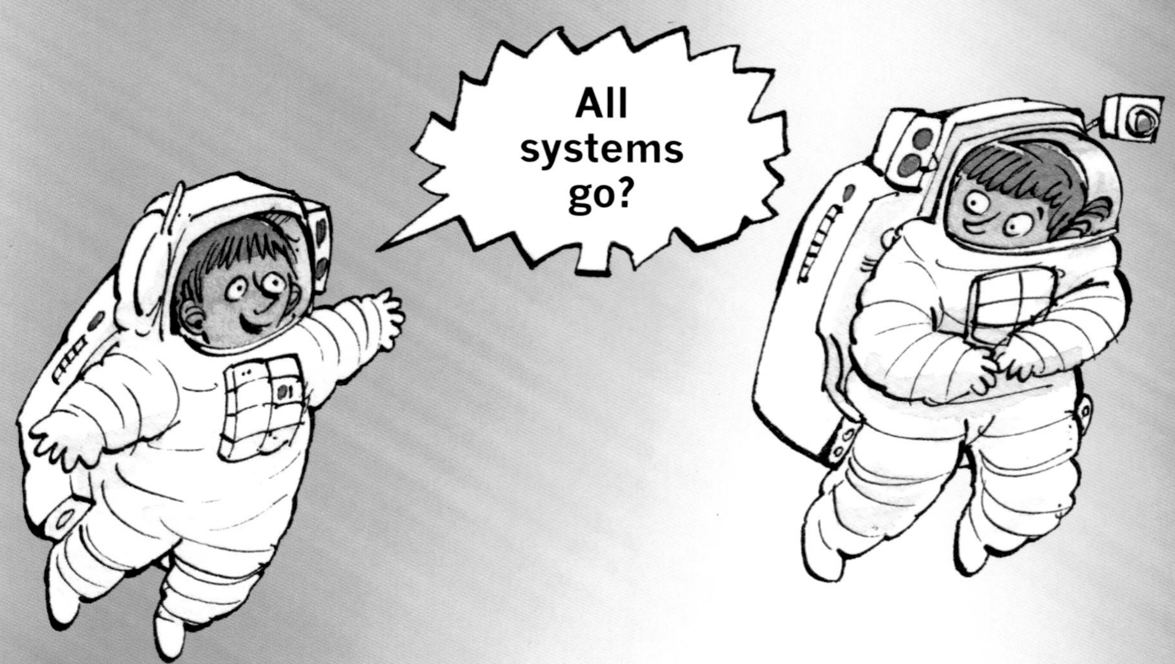

Dave Williams, MD, and Loredana Cunti
art by Theo Krynauw

annick press
toronto + berkeley + vancouver

Quick, take a pic of me with Africa!

Canada

Contents

Poof

Welcome from Dr. Dave

Humans are driven to explore. Our curiosity leads us to ask questions, learn all that we can, and expand our horizons.

Dr. Dave Williams

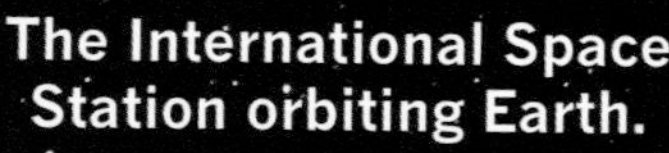

The International Space Station orbiting Earth.

Dr. Dave at work on a space walk

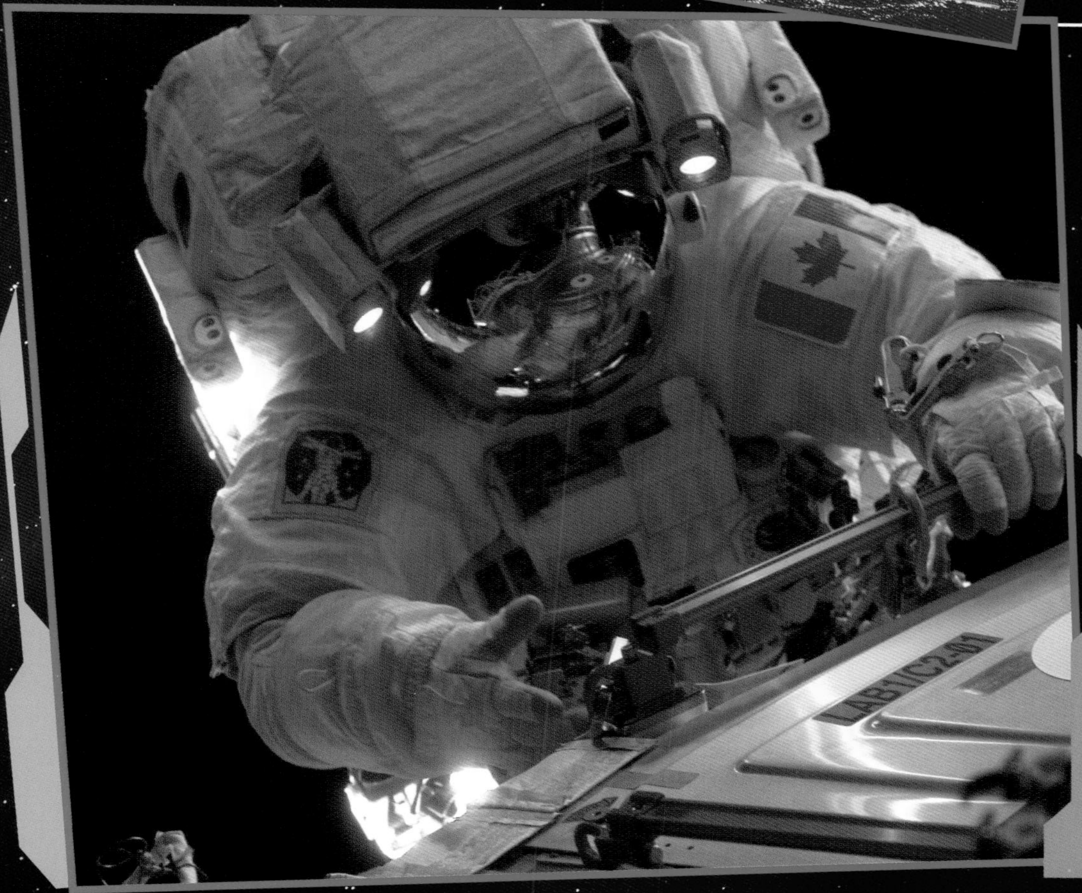

Throughout my career, my curiosity and quest for knowledge have taken me to the depths of the ocean, the frontiers of space, the inner workings of the brain, and a doctor's care for his patients. My passion for science took me on a remarkable journey of discovery in space. As you read this book, I hope you will share in the fun I had on my journey as an explorer and scientist.

—Dr. Dave

What's Up?

Actually, the question we should really be asking is, What's down? The answer: everything, in a world with gravity! All of the amazing things we know about the way our bodies work come from living in a world with gravity—that incredible force that keeps our feet on the ground and everything else from flying off into space. But what happens to the human body when we no longer feel the effects of gravity, at least not in the same way we do on Earth? What happens in space?

The crew of the STS-90 mission

What happens to our bones and our hair? Our appetites and our, um, bodily functions? Do we burp, and fart, and snore like we do on Earth? How do we eat dinner if gravity isn't holding the food on our plates, or our plates on the table? And the number one question astronauts are asked: How do we go to the bathroom?

For astronauts and scientists—and anyone else interested in learning more about life in space—these are important questions, especially if we want to go where no human has gone before.

Flight engineer Clayton C. Anderson at work

All planets have gravity. Planets that are bigger than Earth have a stronger gravitational pull, while planets that are smaller don't have as much.

G Is for G-Force!

Everything on or around Earth is constantly being pulled toward the center of the planet. This force is called gravity, and the unit of measurement used to describe its strength is g-force. Earth's g-force is 1—or 1 g. That 1 g is strong enough to hold down almost everything on the surface of our planet. And whether you live in Australia or America, "down" is toward the center of Earth.

When you go to sleep, you lie down.

When you brush your teeth, you spit down into the sink.

When you jump up in the air, you come back down to the ground.

Zero Gravity? Not Quite

Technically, there is gravity up in space, just very little of it, which is why it's called microgravity. It might not seem like it, but gravity is still at work in an orbiting spacecraft like the International Space Station (ISS). In fact, at the altitude of the ISS, the force of gravity is only 10 percent less than it is on the surface of the earth.

Free Fall

So why do astronauts float around up there? Because we (and the ISS) are in a slow free fall! To stay orbiting around Earth, the ISS has to travel really fast—roughly 25 times faster than the speed of sound. That motion minimizes the pull of gravity, which means the ISS is not falling as fast as, say, a skydiver who jumps from a plane. But it is still falling, and so are the astronauts inside. To prevent the ISS from falling slowly back to Earth over time, visting spacecraft that are attached to the ISS boost it back up to its orbital altitude.

Astronaut Tracy Caldwell Dyson trains for zero gravity in a spin chair

The "Number One" Question

Welcome to Toilet Training

On Earth, we don't even *think* about going to the bathroom. We just do it. But how does it work if you're floating around?

Get the Vacuum Cleaner Out!

Astronauts don't use the P-words (pee or poop). We don't even say "number one" or "number two." We talk about liquid waste and solid waste. And in space, getting rid of waste relies on one important principle: "things" should move away from you.

On Earth, gravity takes care of this for us. But in space, a technological solution is needed to ensure that waste is moving in the right direction—away! Suction to the rescue!

Planetary Plumbing

On the ISS, special toilets use powered airflow or vacuum suction to move waste away from astronauts and into storage compartments. Since the air used to direct the waste is returned to the cabin, it's filtered to control odor and remove any small floating objects. And the waste? Some of that gets reused too. Advanced systems treat and purify liquid waste, turning it into drinking water. Talk about a recycling program!

FUN FACT

Will the houses of the future use this type of water recycling to reduce water demand? Scientists are working to find out.

Practice Makes Perfect

Space toilets look kind of similar to Earth toilets, meaning we can pretty much guess which body part goes where. But watch out! Using a space toilet is not as simple as it looks. Astronauts take part in mandatory training in simulators that imitate what it's like to be in a weightless environment. It takes a lot of practice to make sure things go where they're supposed to and don't get stuck. It's potty training all over again.

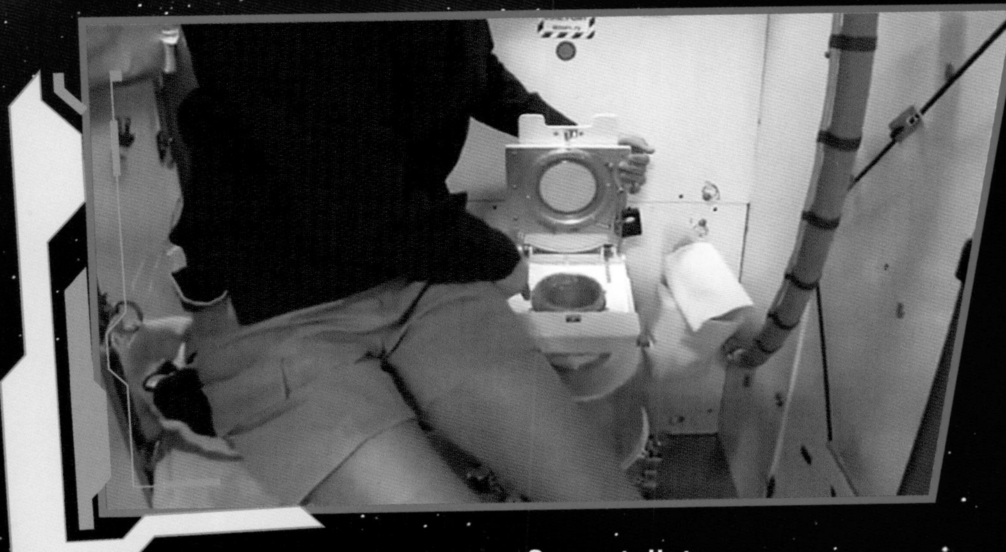

Space toilet

Bathroom Break

Okay, so we know about space toilets and suction. But how does it really work up there when you've got to go? How do you pee in space?

The Proof Is in the Position

It's hard to do your business when you're weightless! That's why space toilets have foot restraints that help us to stay in place. Liquid waste goes directly into a funnel, and the funnel is attached to a urine hose that takes it to the inner workings of the space toilet. If we aim properly, the fans suck in the air and our liquid waste; if we don't, we may have a free-floating mess to clean up.

FUN FACT

Getting the right fit is important! Over the space-exploring years, engineers have developed urine funnels to suit female and male astronauts. On the Space Shuttle program, they were even color-coded to make sure you didn't use your crewmate's by mistake!

Commander Suni Williams shows a bathroom funnel on the ISS

The Countdown

The “T-minus” system is a sequence of backward counting commonly used by NASA to prepare for a rocket launch. Why not use it to countdown to a bathroom break?

P-3

3 Get that airflow going: switch on the WHC (that’s NASA talk for Waste & Hygiene Compartment).

2 Assume the position (remember those foot restraints!).

1 Put your funnel where it needs to be (close but not too close) and …

Ahh! All systems go! Hope you remembered to put the space-station privacy screen in place …

The countdown clock at Kennedy Space Center

Lesson "Number Two"

When it comes to dealing with solid waste, foot restraints alone won't cut it. The opening in the space toilet seat is only 10 centimeters (4 inches) wide; that's smaller than an average grapefruit.

So, once again, positioning is everything.

Hold Me Back ... or Down

Foot restraints, toe loops, seat belts—over the years, space toilets have had a number of features to help keep astronauts in place so we can direct our waste into the suction system and away from our body.

Easier Going

In the past, space toilets weren't nearly as advanced as today's models. The first Apollo astronauts had to use "urine collection devices," bags that would get taped to their ... well, you know where. Awkward! Now, thanks to the airflow system, microgravity bathroom breaks are practically a breeze.

Waste Be Gone!

The average human produces around half a kilogram (1 pound) of solid waste per day. Unlike liquid waste, which can be recycled, solid waste has got to go. The waste gets sucked into a bag that sits inside a metal can, which is sealed once it's full. These cans get put on a cargo module that holds up to 1,700 kilograms (3,748 pounds) of trash! Eventually, the module will burn up when it reenters Earth's atmosphere.

Cosmonaut Yury V. Usachev changes out a solid waste container

Cargo module

Mind Your Manners!

Are you done in there? Shut down the airflow, clean yourself, reset the switches, and clean the space toilet with a bio wipe. Cleaning the WHC after every use is mandatory so it's ready for the next crewmember. And whatever you do, don't break the toilet! There are no plumbers on the mission, so if you break it, you have to fix it yourself. And if you can't, better get those old Apollo bags out!

All Systems Are Slow

So, toilet training is done, right? Not quite. What if things get a bit messy, or don't come out at all?

In a Jam

If you're pushing and pushing without pooping, constipation may be the problem. Whether on Earth or in space, our bodies are constantly losing fluid (through sweat, our breath, and, yes, going to the bathroom). Drinking enough liquid prevents dehydration and keeps our solid waste from getting too hard. What we eat also plays a role in keeping us "regular." Astronauts eat a fiber-rich diet featuring lots of grains and fruit. If that doesn't keep things moving, there are medicines on the space station that can be used to treat constipation.

Cosmonaut Oleg Kotov and astronaut Tracy Caldwell Dyson enjoy their fruits and vegetables

FUN FACT

When it comes to bathroom breaks, bio wipes are an astronaut's best friend. But used wipes are stashed in the solid waste compartment, and since space is so limited, we can't use too many.

Commander Suni Williams shows the bio wipes on the ISS

By the Numbers

We don't often think about how much waste a human body creates, but on the ISS, where there isn't much storage space, it's important to know these things and be prepared to deal with them. On a six-month mission, a crew of six astronauts can produce about 500 kilograms (1,000 pounds) of solid waste and about 2,000 liters (528 gallons) of liquid waste. Depending on the size of the crew, a new solid waste container is needed about every five to ten days.

The Inside Scoop

Here's what astronauts can tell you: walking or floating around the space station is astronomical. But walking and floating around in actual space, with a view of our planet Earth, is literally out of this world! We call this a space walk.

What's Going On Out There?

The technical term for a space walk is Extravehicular Activity (EVA). Space walks are risky business, so they only happen for a few reasons:

- something outside the space station needs to be fixed
- new modules and equipment are being attached to the ISS
- a science experiment needs to be set up

Astronaut Dave Williams works on the ISS during a space walk

Lift-Off Lavatory

A space walk can last between six and eight hours. That's a long time to wait for a bathroom break. So, when it's time to lift off, do a space walk, or reenter Earth's atmosphere, it's back to basics. Time to bust out the Maximum Absorbency Garment (MAG)—better known to Earthlings as a diaper.

Most of us are done with diapers once we learn how to use the toilet. But there aren't any galaxy toilets (that we know of), and even if there were, there's no way we could get out of our pressurized space suits to use them. The bottom line? When you gotta go, you gotta go—so having a piece of equipment that will keep us out in the awesomeness of space for as long as we need to be is MAGnificent.

Astronaut Rick Mastracchio on an EVA

A Mighty Tight Tip

During space-mission training, learning how to use a MAG is a top priority. Keeping "things" contained is pretty important, which means that tightening those waist tabs is extra-important; space is the last place you want to spring a leak!

Clean and Neat

H_2Orbit!

Imagine not having a bath or shower until after your next birthday! That's exactly what would happen if you were on a yearlong mission in outer space. The ISS is equipped with tons of cool stuff, but a shower isn't on the list.

Wild Waterworks

On Earth, the water coming out of a showerhead rolls off your body and goes down the drain. And when you bathe, the water stays in the tub until you pull the drain plug. In the microgravity environment of space all liquids go into free-flow mode—and that's a no-no.

Dr. Dave watches a bubble of tea float freely

Moving Micro Molecules

Water is made up of tiny molecules that are attracted to each other. Because of this attraction (which is called surface tension), loose water droplets will band together in a perfect sphere that floats around until it hits something and sticks to it. Floating water? That's a quick way to ruin all the technological equipment on board the ISS!

FUN FACT

Thanks to surface tension, it's possible for astronauts to "eat" liquid. We can use chopsticks to grab a blob of water, just as if it were solid food. Once it's in our mouths, though, it's back to acting like a liquid. *Gulp*.

Astronaut Takao Doi has fun with a water bubble

Wipe and Swipe

The best way to clean your body in space is with an old-fashioned sponge bath. You'll need a towel and a pouch of soapy water. The pouches come with a straw on the end and could easily be confused with your favorite drink. Stick the straw in, squirt some liquid onto the towel, and start scrubbing. You can towel off the soapy water and then do another round with a little bit of fresh water to rinse.

A Hairy Situation

No showers in space means no hair washing either, right? Sort of. Astronauts use rinseless shampoo to clean their hair. Just put it on, rub it in, and wipe it off with a towel.

Astronaut Tracy Caldwell Dyson tries to brush her hair

The Astro?

You've probably heard of a few famous hairstyles: the mullet, the Bieber, the Beckham, the brush cut. What about the Astro? Like everything else on or in the body, hair is affected by a lack of gravity. In space, long hair floats up off your head, creating the Astro. It's a crazy look, so we use hats and hair bands to keep our locks locked down.

Towel Off

There's no hair dryer on the space station. The filter could easily get clogged with particles, overheat, and cause a fire. Astronauts wisely towel off their hair and then let it air-dry. Our towel allowance? One every other day for bathing, and one every week for basic hygiene. Once used, towels are folded up and stored.

FUN FACT

Don't pack that hair spray! Because styling products make it necessary to wash our hair more often, astronauts don't use them. We save the fancy hairdos for when we get home.

Runaway Hair!

Time for a haircut? An electric clipper attached to a vacuum hose gets the job done and makes sure there are no free-floating pieces of hair for you to breathe in. Brushing regularly will also cut down on runaway hair (and sticky tape is helpful for cleaning your brush).

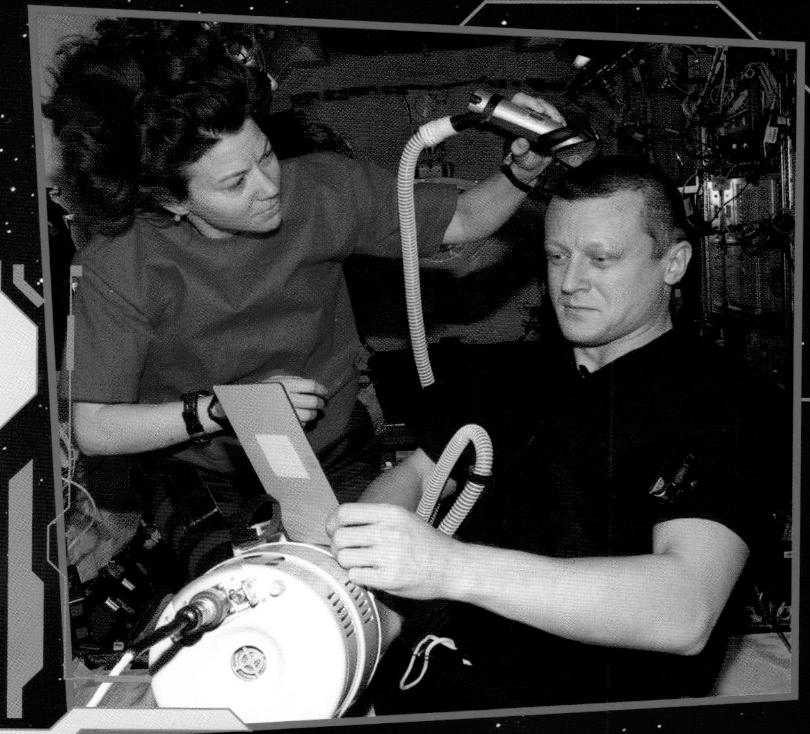

Astronaut Cady Coleman gives cosmonaut Dmitry Kondratyev a haircut

FUN FACT

Our sleep stations contain brushing supplies and a mirror, all stuck to the wall with Velcro, so we can check ourselves out before we start our daily mission.

Free-Floating Fangs

You know the rule: brush your teeth at least every morning and every night. But in space, even that rule needs revising.

The Brief on Brushing

If you were living on the ISS, orbiting Earth and trying to follow your dentist's advice, you'd spend an awful lot of time brushing your teeth. Why? It all comes down to your definition of "morning" and "night." On Earth, it's morning when the sun comes up and night when the sun goes down. In space, things aren't so simple.

The ISS orbits Earth 16 times a day, or once every 90 minutes. That means there's either a sunrise or sunset every 45 minutes. Do the math—you'd end up brushing 32 times a day! Thankfully, astronauts follow a 24-hour Mission Day, in which we stick to the same types of routines as we do on Earth.

Tether Your Toothpaste

With no gravity to help the toothpaste fall onto our brush, we have to squeeze the toothpaste right onto the bristles, making sure none escapes. Then, very carefully (unless we want a face wash too!), we wet a few bristles with a few drops of water from the straw of a drinking bag, and away we go.

So what do you do with a mouthful of used toothpaste in space with no sink? Astronauts use specially designed edible toothpaste, so we can just go ahead and swallow! Ahh, minty fresh!

A water bubble shows the reflection of astronaut Leland Melvin about to wet his toothbrush

FUN FACT

There's no dentist on the ISS, so astronauts get a full checkup just before flight to try to make sure there won't be any problems in space.

Go Blow!

Picking your nose is astronaut-approved. Seriously.

What the Nose Knows

The nose has many functions:

- It allows us to smell and breathe.
- It warms and humidifies the air we breathe.
- The hairs inside keep foreign objects out of our respiratory system.

Pesky Particles

On Earth, nose hairs trap the odd particle here and there, but many of those bits and pieces just fall to the floor where they collect and eventually become dust bunnies. In space, though, dust bunnies float! Although there are (literally) tons of fans to keep the air circulating and filters to suck up those loose airborne particles, some still escape. And those that do will get into every available opening—including your nostrils! They float right onto your nose hairs, and that's where they get stuck.

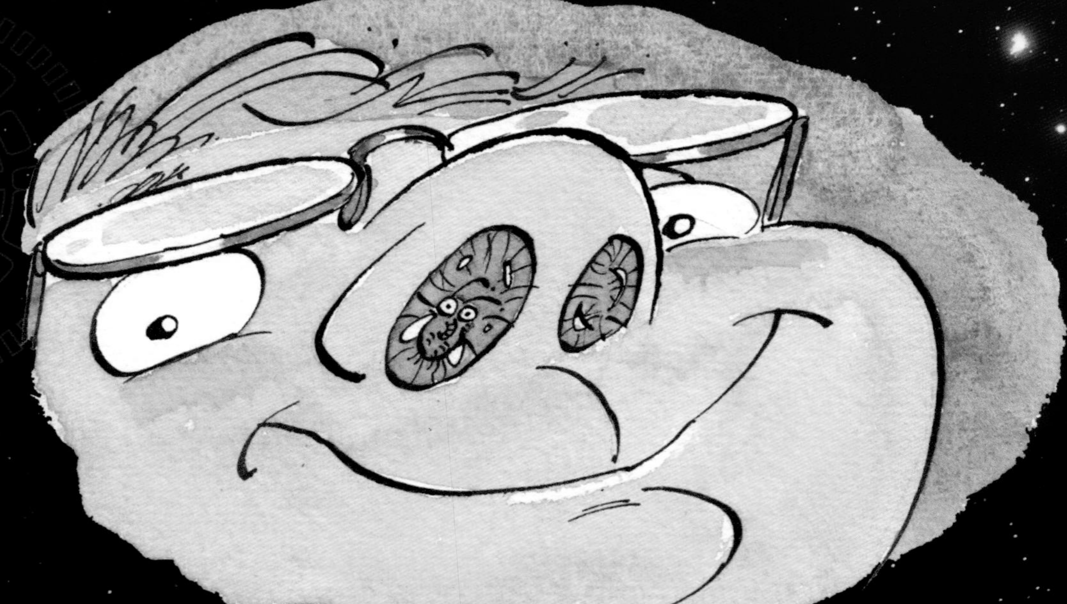

Digital Extraction

When something's stuck in your nose, what do you do? Go blow, right? It's a good first step, but after a few attempts to politely dislodge micro-sized specks of scrambled eggs and lint, all astronauts come to the realization that the only practical solution is digital extraction.

Digital Extraction = Picking Your Nose

Yes, forget all those lectures about not picking your nose; in space, you're good to go! It's best to make it part of your daily hygiene, though you might want to pull back that privacy screen. There are lots of cameras on the space station!

Astronauts Barbara Morgan, Alvin Drew (center), and Clayton Anderson ready their cameras on the ISS

All Dressed Up

Whatever Suits You

One of the best things about being an astronaut is getting to wear your space suit—or Extravehicular Mobility Unit (EMU), in NASA-speak. Space suits are like personalized mini-spacecraft. All systems are working hard to keep you comfortable on your space walk.

EMU!

Extravehicular = outside the space station
Mobility = the astronaut can move around out in space
Unit = because it sounds cool

FUN FACT

Putting a space suit on is called donning. Removing the suit is called doffing.

Why Is a Space Suit White?

On a hot day on Earth, wearing white reflects the heat from the sun, which allows us to stay cool. White space suits work the same way, reflecting heat that can reach a toasty 135° Celsius (275° Fahrenheit) in the direct sunlight of space. Good thing there's an in-suit drink bag! Each one contains 1 liter (4 cups) of water.

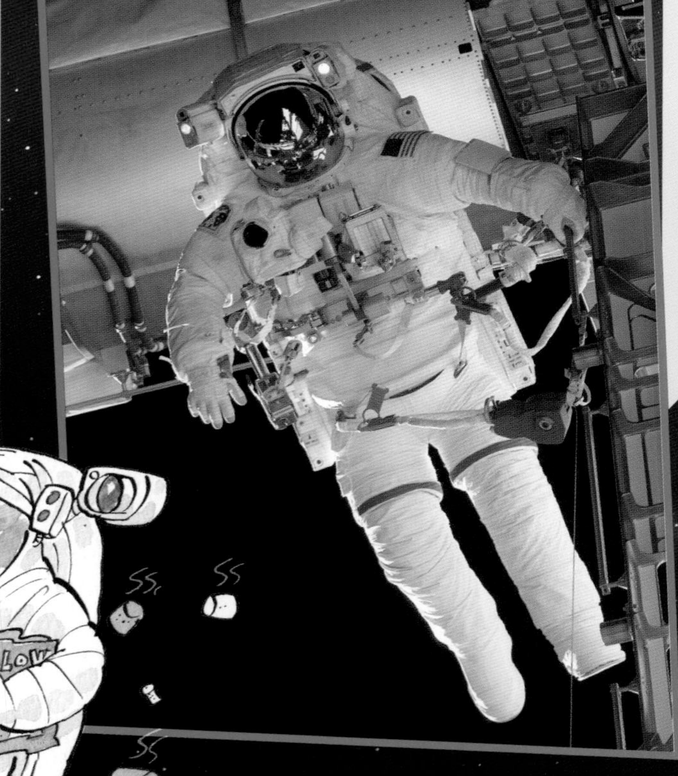

Astronaut Rick Mastracchio performs a task outside the ISS

Space Suit To-Do List

- ✔ Monitor suit pressure
- ✔ Monitor suit oxygen
- ✔ Monitor suit CO^2
- ✔ Monitor battery level

Heavy Duty

The typical EMU weighs about 127 kilograms (280 pounds). And astronauts going out on an EVA also carry between 70 and 110 kilograms of tools and other pieces of equipment. Combined, it's like carrying a female lion on your back. Thankfully, in space, that's featherweight.

FUN FACT

The controls in your space suit help you stay comfy on your space walk. The suit's cooling system gets rid of the heat produced by your body, but if you get too cold, you can turn it off to warm up.

Dr. Dave busy at work outside the ISS

Cosmic Clothing

Space walks, exercise training, daily scientific experiments—there are so many things to dress for on a mission to space! What do you pack?

Fashion in Flight

Astronauts wear regular, comfortable mission clothing when they are on board the ISS accomplishing their daily missions of science and space experiments. We choose our shirts and pants way ahead of when we'll be wearing them, and since there is no washing machine up there, we don't change clothes as often as we do here on Earth.

Astronaut Barbara Morgan in comfortable mission clothing

Galactic Undies

Astronauts got very excited when the Japanese space agency developed new underwear made of a special antibacterial fabric that helps reduce the spread of bacteria. One astronaut supposedly wore the same pair for a whole month without any complaints about the smell (usually, we change undies every three days). Either the new underwear work, or that crew was just really polite!

Working Up a Sweat

In order to keep their bones and muscles strong, astronauts exercise up to two hours a day in space. But the space station isn't a typical gym. Harnesses are needed to keep us on the exercise equipment, and here, no one wants to see you sweat. In fact, keeping sweat away from your body—and from everything else—means wearing dedicated exercise shirts and shorts that absorb sweat.

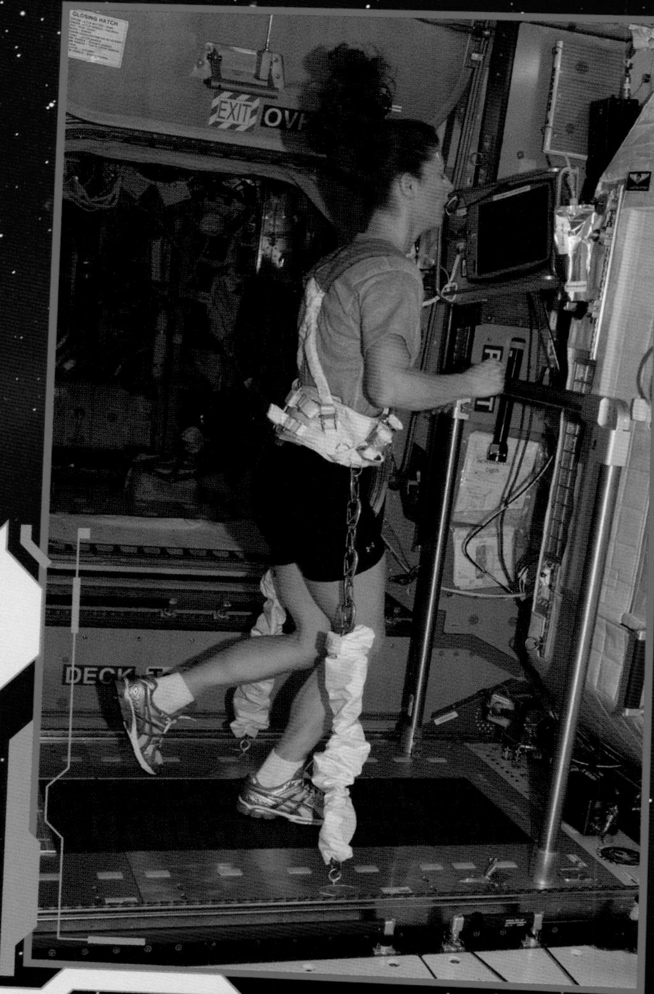

Astronaut Tracy Caldwell Dyson exercises on the ISS

FUN FACT

Astronauts in the Russian space program are called *cosmonauts* and astronauts in the Chinese space program are called *taikonauts*.

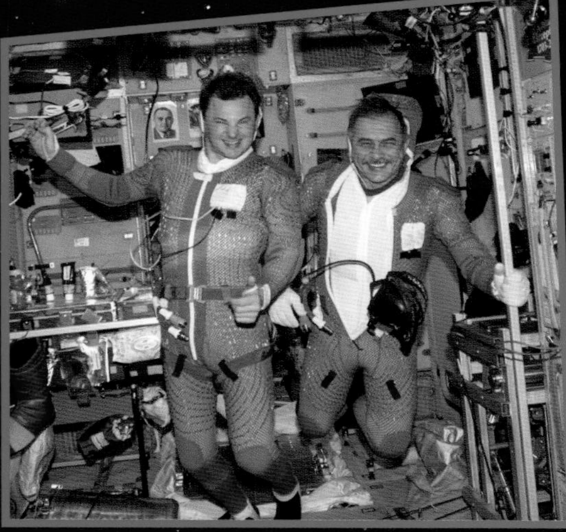

Cosmonauts Roman Romanenko (left) and Pavel Vinogradov

Shake It Off?

What if you decided to skip the special exercise shirt? Well, sweat would form a pool on your chest and back. As much as you might be tempted … DO NOT shake. Have you ever run away from a wet dog shaking water out of its fur? That's how you can expect your crewmates to treat you!

Antigravity Appetite

Let's Eat!

Free-floating is one of the best feelings in the world—except when it makes you want to toss your cookies. Some astronauts get motion sickness at first, kind of like that feeling you get when you're on a giant roller coaster. This can make you avoid eating a lot in the first few days of a mission.

Hunger in the Habitat

By the time you've been in space for a few days, your appetite has almost fully returned. In some cases, you might be less hungry in space than down on Earth, because whatever you do eat or drink seems to move more slowly through your digestive system, making you feel fuller for longer.

Astronaut Rick Mastracchio enjoys a tortilla

Camp Cosmos

A mission in outer space is kind of like camping: everything you eat and drink has to get shipped up from Earth and is picked well in advance. This means the menu is not exactly huge and doesn't leave room for cravings. A team of food scientists makes sure that the specially formulated food available on the space station has all the nutrients an astronaut needs, is compact (so it can be stored in the limited pantry space), nonperishable, and super-tasty.

Thanksgiving Day

Irradiated smoked turkey
Thermostabilized candied yams
Freeze-dried green beans
Freeze-dried mushrooms
Freeze-dried corn-bread dressing
Thermostabilized cherry-blueberry cobbler

The Nonperishable Pantry

Freeze-dried: astronaut has to add water
Thermostabilized: foods have been heat-processed to destroy bacteria so they can be stored at room temperature
Powdered: astronaut has to add hot or cold water to beverages
Irradiated: foods have been treated with a technology designed to get rid of parasites and other bacteria

Grab That Fork!

Like you and your family, astronauts eat together. It's a good time to share stories—and to practice our free-floating food skills. With everything floating in microgravity, utensils, food cans, sauces, and seasonings like salt and pepper must all be fastened to the walls or a surface nearby—though that won't stop your fork from floating out of your hand!

Cosmonaut Yuri Malenchenko (left) and astronaut Edward Lu share a meal

Terrestrial Taste

What we taste when we eat comes from both the smell of the food and the way that food stimulates the taste buds on our tongues. Our taste buds are sensitive to four basic types of flavor: sweet, sour, salty, and bitter.

Does This Taste Different to You?

The taste of food in space is different from the taste of food on the ground. It's not that food tastes bad, it's just that it tastes … less. For some astronauts, the bland blahs improve as the mission goes on, but for others, the sensation lasts for the entire mission.

Why? No one knows for sure, but one theory is that the smell of all the other things in the space station competes with the smell of the food and dulls the taste. Another theory is that fluid changes in the body cause nasal congestion, limiting our ability to smell and, therefore, our ability to taste. Whatever the reason, astronauts like to spice their food up with lots of sauce.

Astronaut Koichi Wakata prepares to eat with his chopsticks

STS-131 and Expedition 23 crew members enjoy a meal together

Spice in Space

The ISS food pantry stocks lots of different flavorings like ketchup, mustard, hot chili sauce, wasabi, and liquid salt and pepper. As a treat, astronauts get to send up a small amount of their favorite food in the cargo. Caribou jerky, anyone?

FUN FACT

Watch the squirt! Squirting out floating sauce is a special skill, known only to astronauts!

To Burp or Not to Burp?

So, you've eaten your space food and now you feel a burp coming on. Forget about it. Burping in space is too high risk. What? Sure, burping is considered to be less than polite, but high risk?

Burps for Beginners

You sometimes burp after you've had certain foods and drinks, like cabbage or bubbly carbonated beverages. You might also burp after eating too fast. Why? Because a lot of air gets swallowed with your food. A burp is just air, or gas, looking to get out.

On Earth, gravity causes liquids and food to sit at the bottom of your stomach, while air sits on top. When there's too much air, your stomach opens a little gate to the tube that runs between your stomach and your mouth. *Whoosh*—out goes the air!

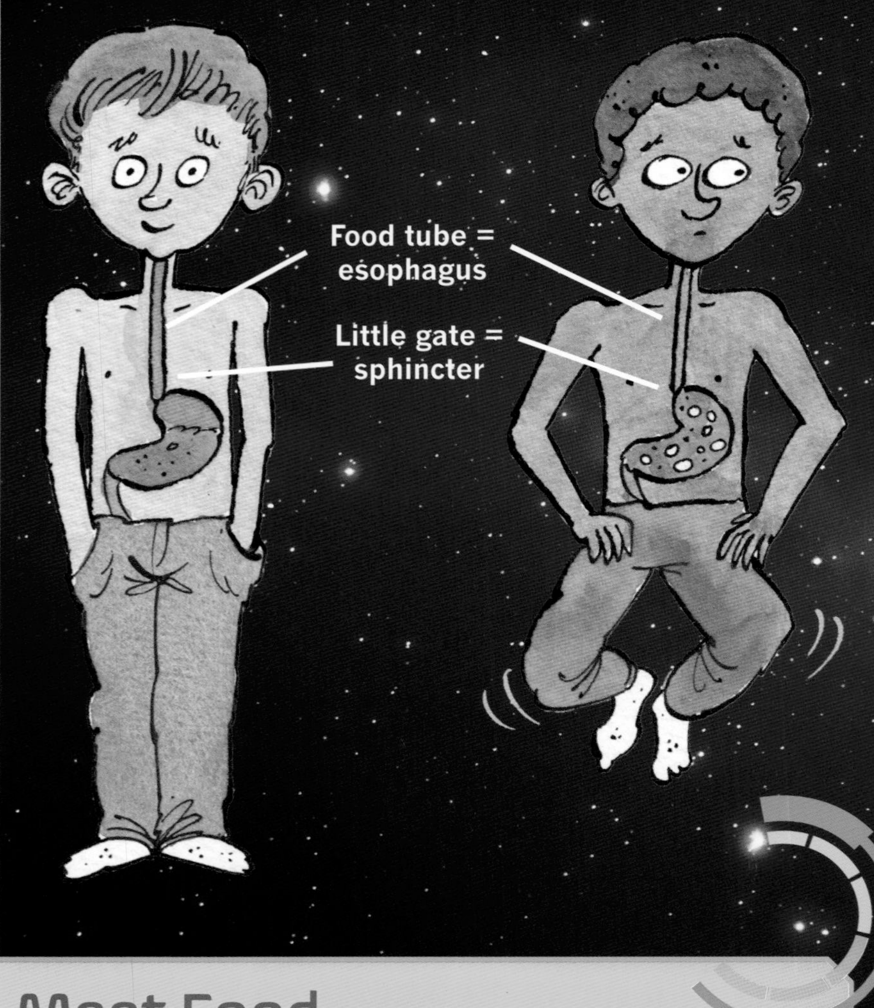

Air, Meet Food

In the microgravity of space, the air in your stomach does not conveniently separate from the food. Instead, it's blended in with all of your stomach contents—chicken teriyaki meets burrito meets peach ambrosia (an all-time favorite astronaut dessert) meets air. There's a lot going on down there in your gut!

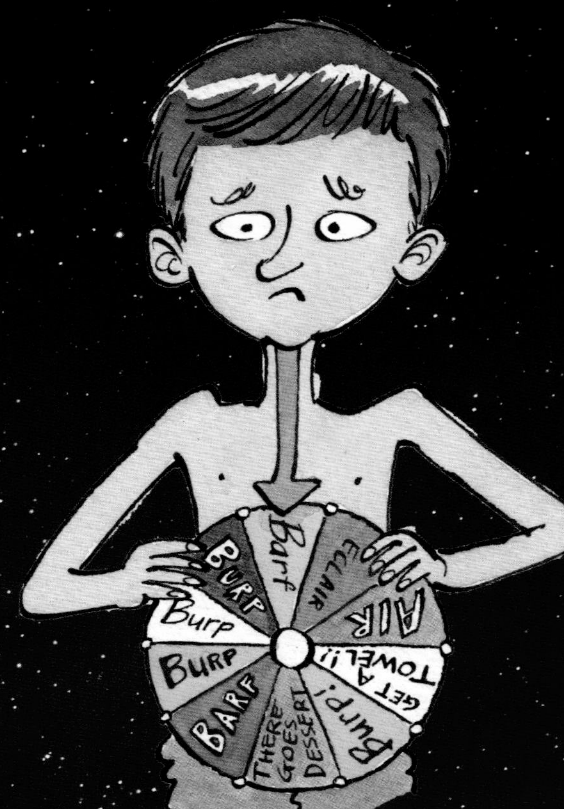

Burp at Your Own Risk

On Earth, we can sense whether we are going to burp or whether we are about to throw up. In space, if you want to take a chance on a burp, just know that there's no predicting what's going to come out! It could be a harmless bit of digestive gas, or it could be the remnants of lunch. Whatever the outcome, be prepared to swallow quickly, or make sure you have a cleanup plan ready!

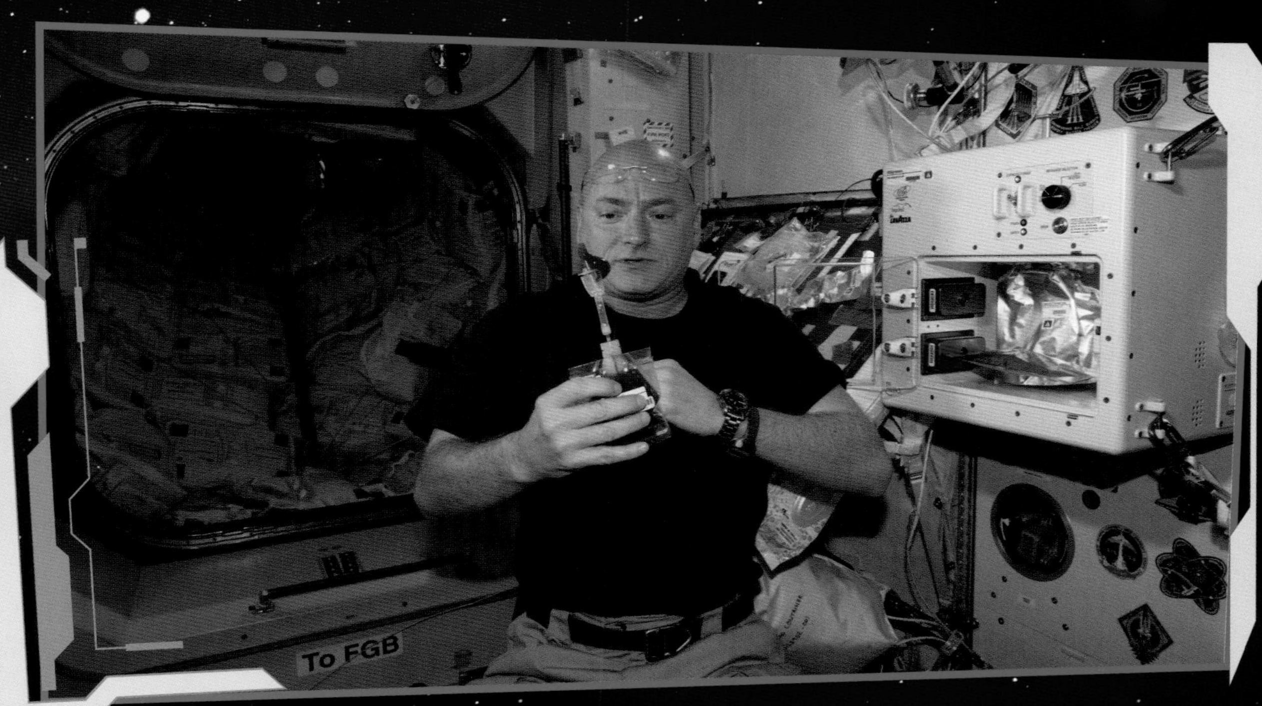

Astronaut Scott Kelly tastes his first drink from the new ISSpresso machine

What's That Smell?

A toot. Hot wind. A fart. Whatever you want to call it, it's digestive gas. But what happens when you pass gas in space?

Facts on Flatulence

Farts are either the result of swallowed air or of gas produced when food is digested. Some foods are particularly prone to creating gas.

Gases in farts like hydrogen, nitrogen, and methane do not make farts smelly.

Fancy-sounding chemicals like sulfides, indoles, and methanethiols are the stinky ones.

All Systems Are Blow

Farting is a fact of life, so if you've really got to do it on board, just be sure to hang out by one of the filters so the fan can deal with it. Or you can wait until you're in the privacy of your own space suit. Hopefully your visor won't fog up!

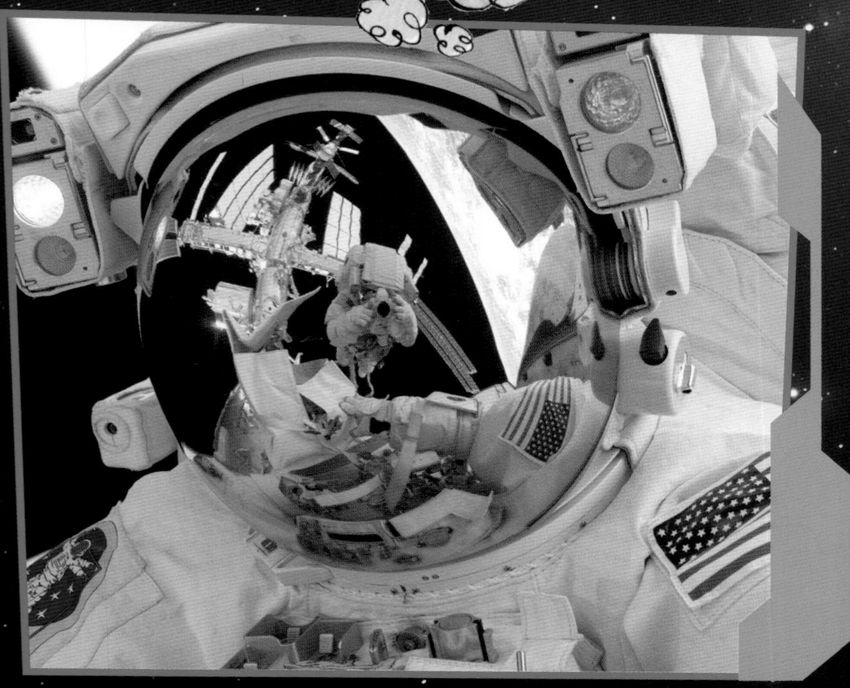

Astronaut Ron Garan's reflection on the helmet of Mission Specialist Mike Fossum

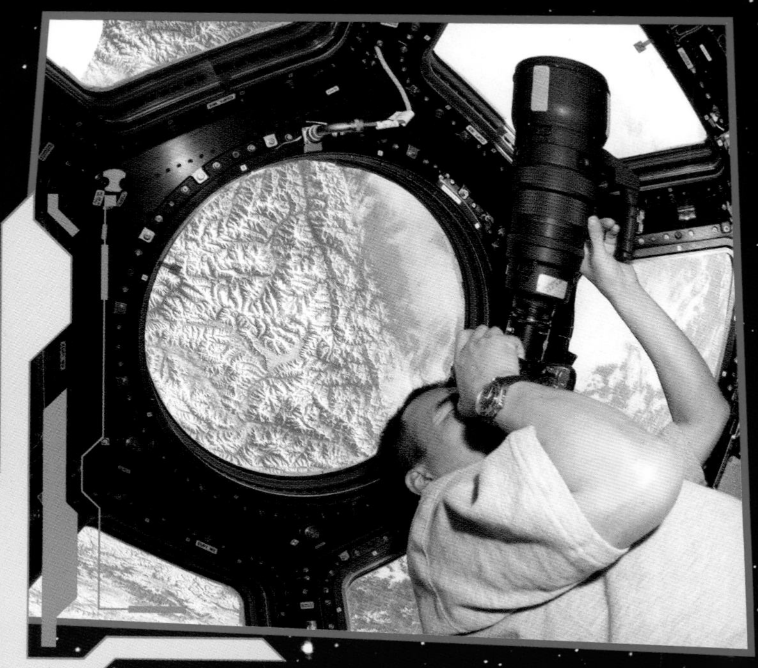

Nose, Beware!

There's no evidence that farts smell worse in space than on Earth. But with all those smelly chemicals floating around and no windows that open on your spacecraft to let the air escape, you probably want to avoid eating too much broccoli.

Astronaut Soichi Noguchi captures shots of Earth from the windows of the Cupola

Grocery List for Gas

Cabbage
Carbonated drinks
Cauliflower
(And that's just the *C*s)

Human-Powered Jet Pack?

Crazy thought: With all that "gas" power from a fart, can astronauts self-propel? Nope. Even if we're weightless, we can't go from blast to blastoff since the propulsive effect of a fart could never offset our body mass.

Body Basics

Going to Your Head

By now, you're getting the sense that life in space isn't at all like life on Earth. Things taste different. Toilets and showers are different. You even have to burp more carefully. Why wouldn't you look different too?

Hello, Moon-face!

As soon as you arrive in space, you'll feel your face getting puffy. When you look in the mirror, don't be surprised. Yes, your face *is* bigger! This is a direct result of living in microgravity. Astronauts develop what space doctors might call "puffy moon-face bird-leg syndrome."

Going Up?

The human body is about 60 percent water. Normally, that water is distributed throughout your upper and lower body. In space, though, the water shifts. In fact, this is one of the first changes that take place once you leave Earth. The fluids that normally reside in your lower extremities (like your legs, hips, ankles) redistribute throughout your upper body (your arms, chest, head). More water in your head means puffy moon-face; less water in your lower body means bird-leg syndrome.

Pros and Cons

Pros

- Wrinkles disappear.
- Everything gets less puffy over the first few weeks of the space flight and goes back to normal once you're on Earth again.

Cons

- The extra fluid in your head produces nasal congestion, and you can feel like you have a cold.
- When you video call from space, friends and family wonder why you look so strange.

Astronauts Julie Payette and Robert Thirsk adjust to changes on the ISS

The Long and Short of It

Most of us stop growing sometime in our teens. Not astronauts! Our bodies can grow up to 5 centimeters (2 inches) in space. Good news for our slam-dunks!

Building Blocks

Your backbone, or spine, is made of 24 bones called vertebrae, stacked on top of each other like blocks from your pelvis to the bottom of your skull. Vertebrae are separated by discs that act like little shock absorbers. They protect the bones from hitting each other and also help absorb the impact of jumping up and down.

The Incredible Shrinking Kid

As you've learned, gravity has a number of effects on the human body. Here's a big one: it actually makes us shorter. Those discs in your spine are composed mainly of water. When you stand, run, walk, or play, gravity compresses the discs. On an average day, you could lose about 1 percent of your height between your morning alarm and lights-out. The good news? Lying down for a good night's sleep ensures that you regain that height by the time you wake up the next day.

Crop Tops on Board

In space, where gravity isn't up to its usual tricks, the disc space between vertebrae gets bigger. Our bodies lengthen, and we're actually taller for the entire flight. No need to rush out and buy new pants, though. The lengthening happens in your spine, and your height goes back to normal as soon as you stand up on Earth.

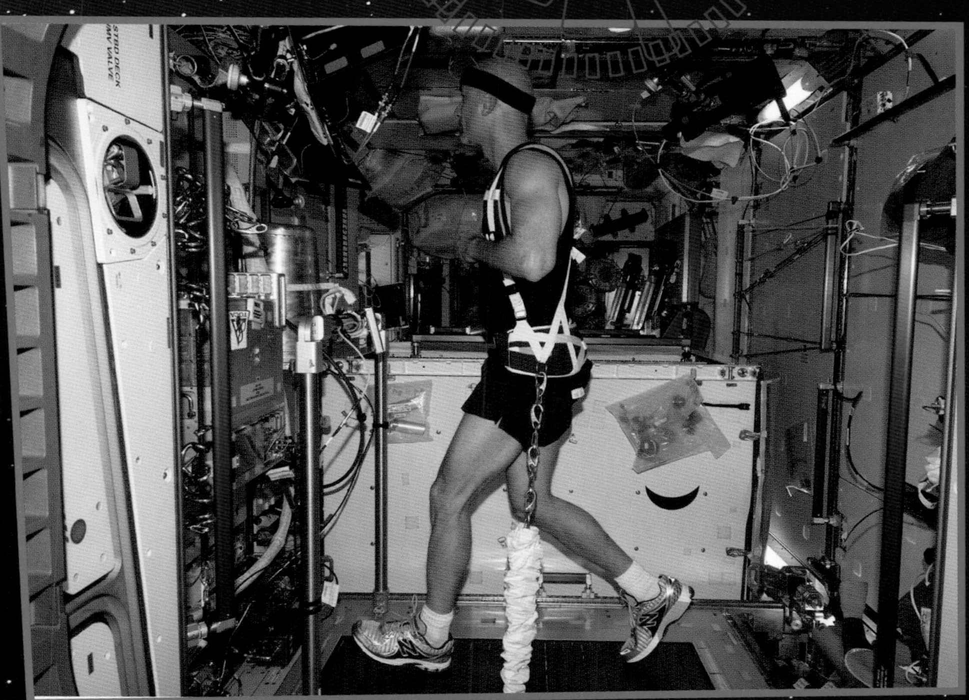

Astronaut Luca Parmitano's height returned to normal once he was back on Earth

It's Alive!

When you think of a skeleton, you probably think of something dead. It's just a rack of bones, after all, a place to hang muscles and skin so we look like a person and not something out of a horror movie. News flash: bones are alive, and they play a vital role in helping our bodies function on Earth.

Game of Bones

Osteoblasts are the cells that create new bone, and *osteoclasts* are the cells that remove it. On Earth, these cells are constantly building and breaking down bone, responding to the stress and forces applied by day-to-day activities. But what happens when a bigger-than-usual stress occurs, like when we break a bone? Without the builder cells, the bone wouldn't heal. And if the builder cells don't work properly, your bone density—or bone strength—decreases, and you can break a bone much more easily than usual. Ouch!

Working Hard or Hardly Working?

With much less gravity working against them, bones experience much less stress in space than on Earth. A space mission is kind of like a holiday for the bone builders, so they take a bit of a break. But the bone removers aren't the sitting-around-on-the-beach type. They're happy to keep on working, reabsorbing bone material. The result? Astronauts start to lose bone density—in some cases at a rate of between 2 and 3 percent of their bone density per month. They also lose muscle mass, which leads to decreased strength and can reduce an astronaut's ability to do work. That's why there's no holiday from exercise for an astronaut!

Dr. Dave hard at work

Planet Jellyfish?

If you were in space for a couple of years, would you eventually resorb all of your bones and turn into a jellyfish? No, but you would lose a significant amount of bone density. Once back on Earth, you'd have to be very careful to avoid fractures. With time and exercise, however, the osteoblasts would get blasting again, and your bone density would return.

Space Flight Nighty-Night

Sleeping in Space

Teeth brushed? Check. Pajamas on? Check. Pillow fluffed? Not quite. In space, there are no pillows. Because there are no beds. Because there is no lying down.

Drifting Off

There are six sleeping pods on the ISS, and each is about the size of your closet at home. The sleep restraint system—also known as a sleeping bag—is attached to the wall of the sleep pod, and most astronauts choose to sleep inside the bag. But because there is no up or down in space, any sleeping position will work. Astronauts in need of a short nap often just close their eyes and drift … literally … off.

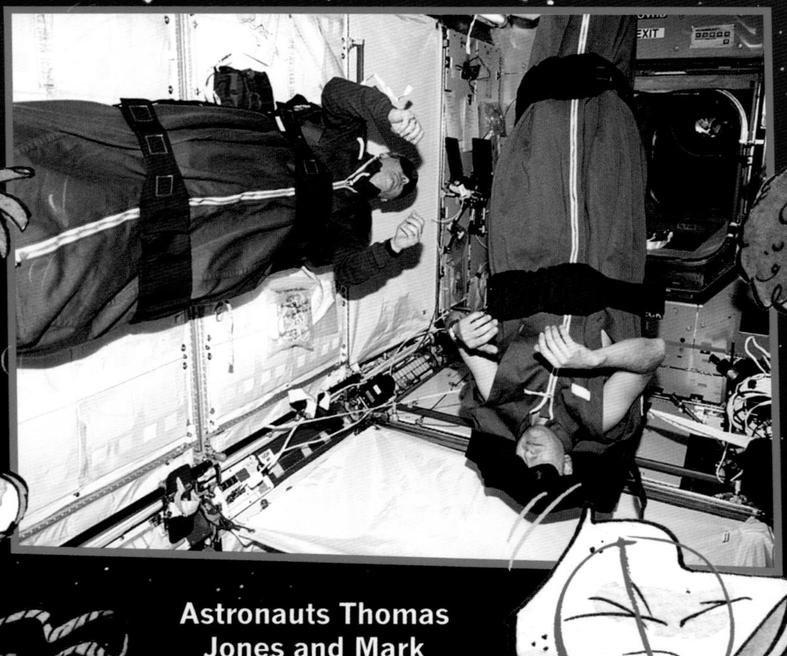

Astronauts Thomas Jones and Mark Polansky during their sleep shifts

Zombies in Orbit!

Don't be startled if you wake up in the middle of the night with a pair of arms floating in front of you—they're yours! Sleeping with your arms outside of your sleeping bag creates a zombie-like look, but it's actually the natural position of the arms without gravity. Your hips and knees bend a bit too, making it really easy to relax and fall asleep.

Astronaut Samantha Cristoforetti in her sleeping bag

Pass the Earplugs

Sleep helps our bodies and brains develop and grow. So should snorers who disrupt your sleep be sent to space? Yes! On Earth, when a snorer is sleeping, the muscles in the mouth and throat relax. Gravity causes the muscles to fall toward the back of the throat, creating a partial blockage of the air passage to the lungs. Smoothly flowing air is silent. Air flowing over an obstacle is not! Be warned: a stubborn snorer might still make a little noise in space, but the noisy fans will block some of the racket.

Our Bodies Beyond—What's Next?

Our bodies are pretty awesome. We can adapt to live in extreme cold and hot climates, in high-altitude regions, and at sea level. This is all part of living in a world with gravity.

With a few important adjustments and some amazing technology, we can adapt to living in a world with much less gravity. Astronauts have been traveling to and living in outer space for some time now. And space agencies will keep on studying and learning more about what happens to our bodies while we are exploring our incredible solar system.

NASA's Mars rover vehicle, Curiosity

Go Farther and Stay Longer!

Did you know it takes six months just to get to Mars? And that doesn't include being there and coming back! Doctors, scientists, technology experts, engineers, and mathematicians have a lot of questions to answer about how to keep humans fit and healthy as we explore farther and stay longer.

What exercises will make sure our bones and muscles stay strong for so long in microgravity?

What equipment and clothing will protect the human body from the radiation and elements of outer space on such a long journey?

What activities and experiments can we integrate into the day-to-day life on a small spaceship to help keep astronauts from getting bored?

Now that we know that water exists on Mars, space scientists are working on answering these questions and others. ("Does life on Mars really exist?")

The goal is to someday send humans to the red planet to search for signs of life. Will they find any? Let's keep exploring to find out!

FURTHER READING

Branley, Franklyn M. (Author), and Kelley, True (Illustrator). *Floating in Space*, HarperCollins, 1998.

Branley, Franklyn M. (Author), and Edward Miller (Illustrator). *Gravity Is a Mystery*. HarperCollins, 2007.

Branley, Franklyn M. (Author), and Kelley, True (Illustrator). *The International Space Station.* HarperCollins, 2000.

Braun, Eric (Author), and Harmer, Sharon (Illustrator). *If I Were an Astronaut (Dream Big!)*. Picture Window Books, 2009.

Brubaker Bradley, Kimberly (Author), and Meisel, Paul (Illustrator). *Forces Make Things Move.* HarperCollins, 2005.

Hughes, Catherine D. (Author) and Aguilar, David A. (Illustrator). *National Geographic Little Kids First Big Book of Space*: National Geographic Kids, 2012.

Mullane, R. Mike. *Do Your Ears Pop in Space? And 500 Other Surprising Questions About Space Travel.* Wiley, 1997.

ONLINE RESOURCES

CANADIAN SPACE AGENCY
www.asc-csa.gc.ca/eng/educators

EUROPEAN SPACE AGENCY — Space for Kids
www.esa.int/esaKIDSen

NASA KIDS CLUB
www.nasa.gov/audience/forkids/kidsclub/flash

IMAGE CREDITS

The appearance of any persons in this book in no way means to imply their endorsement. The inclusion of NASA material in no way means to imply any endorsement by NASA. The photographs on the following pages are used courtesy of NASA (additional credits below): **2, 3 top and bottom, 4, 5, 9, 10, 13 left and right, 14, 15, 16, 17, 18, 19, 20, 21, 22 top and bottom, 23, 25, 26 and back cover, 27, 28, 29 left and right, 30, 31, 32, 33, 35, 37, 39, 41, 43, 44, 45. Front cover main image,** © Leonello Calvetti/Stocktrek Images; **cartoon rocket used on front cover and title page,** © Dhimas Ronggobramantyo/Dreamstime.com; **metal background used throughout as on title page,** © Mamakestudio/Dreamstime.com; **moon background used throughout as on table of contents,** © Dvmsimages/Dreamstime.com; **gears used throughout as on table of contents,** © Anawhite/Dreamstime.com; **arrows used throughout as on 2,** © Dtvector/Dreamstime.com; **night sky used as background throughout as on 2,** © PixelParticle/Dreamstime.com; **futuristic frames, graphic half circles and power bars used throughout as on 2 and 4,** © Shadow_cluster/Dreamstime.com; **whole graphic circles used throughout as on page 2 and in chapter numbers,** © Alex Ciopata/Dreamstime.com; **sunrise on planet Earth from space used throughout as on 4,** (excepting elements courtesy NASA): © Denisismagilov/Dreamstime.com; **solar system used throughout as on 5,** © Alhovik/Dreamstime.com; **7,** courtesy NASA/Victor Zelentsov; **11,** courtesy NASA/Jim Grossmann; **22 middle,** © Connect1/Dreamstime.com; **36,** courtesy NASA/JSC; **46,** courtesy NASA/JPL-Caltech/MSSS; **47,** detail of artwork by Pat Rawlings, of SAIC, courtesy NASA.

INDEX

Cover design by Sheryl Shapiro
Edited by Linda Pruessen
Designed by Sheryl Shapiro

Annick Press Ltd.

We acknowledge the support of the Canada Council for the Arts, the Ontario Arts Council, and the participation of the Government of Canada/la participation du gouvernement du Canada for our publishing activities.

Funded by the Government of Canada
Financé par le gouvernement du Canada

Cataloging in Publication
Williams, Dafydd, 1954–, author
To burp or not to burp : a guide to your body in space /
Dr. Dave Williams and Loredana Cunti.

(Dr. Dave Astronaut)
Issued in print and electronic formats.
ISBN 978-1-55451-854-8 (hardback).—ISBN 978-1-55451-853-1 (paperback).—
ISBN 978-1-55451-855-5 (epub).—ISBN 978-1-55451-856-2 (pdf)
1. Space flight—Physiological effect—Juvenile literature. I. Cunti, Loredana, 1968-, author II. Title. III. Series: Williams, Dafydd, 1954– . Dr. Dave Astronaut.

RC1150.W55 2016 j612'.0145 C2016-901879-2
C2016-901880-6

Published in the U.S.A. by Annick Press (U.S.) Ltd.
Distributed in Canada by University of Toronto Press.
Distributed in the U.S.A. by Publishers Group West.

Printed in China

Visit us at: www.annickpress.com

Also available in e-book format. Please visit www.annickpress.com/ebooks.html for more details.
Or scan

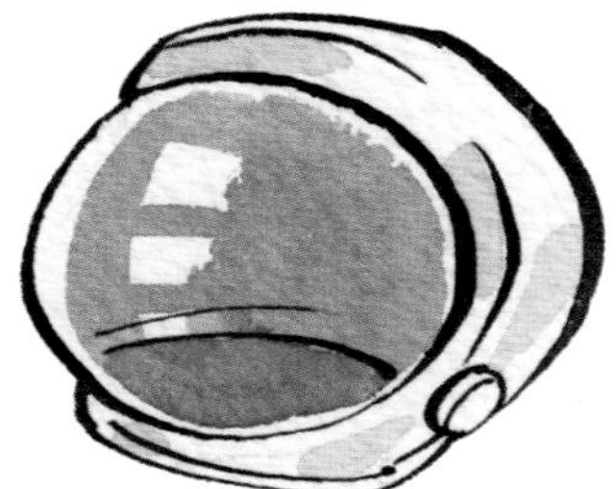

This book is dedicated to my family for their support and encouragement, to my parents who taught me the importance of lifelong learning, and to the next generation of physicians, scientists, explorers, and those who dream of furthering the quest for knowledge. —D.W.

To Vienna and Frederick. For believing I might still be able to blast off to outer space. —L.C.